The Village

The war and the occupation through
the eyes of a four-year-old

Magda Demou-Gryparis

The Village

The war and the occupation through the eyes of a four-year-old

A True Story

by Magda Demou-Gryparis

OCEANPUBLICATIONS

General Layout/Cover: OceanPublications
Publisher: Maria Pappa
Editing by Katalina Gerasopoulou
Printing/Binding: Create Space
All Rights reserved Magda Demou-Gryparis
Published Florida, USA – 2017

OceanPublications
www.oceanpublications.us
oceanpublications@gmail.com

Dedication

To my grandchildren August, Corin, Aiden, and Loghan.

Magda Demou-Gryparis

Acknowledgements

I want to thank my publisher Maria Pappa who believed in this book from the beginning and worked with me patiently and tirelessly to fulfill my dream. I also thank all the people at Ocean Publications for their fine work.

I owe gratitude to Ilias Nellas the editor of Rovoliaritika Nea (Rovoliari News) who loved my story. His suggestions, ideas, and information on the village life were valuable. He translated my English draft into Greek and published it in the Village newspaper. There would not be a book today without him.

I thank my family and my two children Mark and Katerina who thought they had heard the story all through their childhood they still read it and supported my effort.

My son Mark who pointed out that although this was just another war story, still it was different because it was written from a child's point of view.

My daughter Katerina who worked together with Maria Pappa setting up my business side of writing, not a favorite subject of mine.

I thank my grandson Corin, the future film maker, for his enthusiasm and for his promise to put my story into a film someday.

Thank you to my 13-year-old grandson Aiden who read my early draft and pointed out that my story needed a prologue and came to my rescue on computer issues. He is a fine technical support instructor.

I thank my dear husband who has been my support and my rock through all this. Demetri thank you for the delicious dinners.
I thank my friend Laure Ebner who enjoyed reading my early draft.

And last but not least, I want to thank my good friend Ruth Jensen who spent hours working with me on the fine points of editing and grammar on the final draft.

Magda Demou-Gryparis

Prologue

She walked slowly to her comfortable, easy chair leaning heavily on her cane and sat down to rest her painful body. Her back was stiff and throbbing. She rested her head and closed her eyes trying to relax. It was a long and busy day. She over-exerted herself.
It was not every day that you turn 80 years old; she told herself.

She glanced at the recliner in front of the television set where Anthony her dear husband and life companion of 58 years was sleeping with his mouth open, snoring quietly. It was a tiring day for him also, despite his loud announcements, "I am young and beautiful. I can do anything."

Their two children insisted that their parents should have a party to celebrate her big day.
"We'll do everything Mama," they said.
"We'll plan it so you and Dad will not have to do anything."

So, all the family gathered in the small but comfortable apartment.

It was a joyful celebration. Their two children, their spouses and the four grandchildren grown up now, with them, all together in one room. It was a rare but special occasion.

She blew out the multicolored candles on her white frosted cake and they all clapped cheerfully wishing her Happy Birthday.
She sat looking at her beloved family around her with a proud smile on her face, her heart brimming with love for them.
Her happiness was complete.

Alex, 24 years old, her oldest grandson, came up and sat next to her. He leaned over and gave her a warm hug.
He took her hands in his and asked, "How are you feeling these days Grandma? Sorry I don't come to see you more often. I am too busy with school and work. You know how it is." "Grandma" he continued, "Are you in a lot of pain?
"Oh, the usual Alex. I have my good days and my bad days,"
She smiled, "You know, old bones cannot be mended and become young again."
"Grandma, I wanted to ask you. Dad mentioned once that you lived through a horrendous experience during the last war when you were very young in the old country, Greece. How old were you then? Do you remember anything?"

"Yes, my boy I do remember. No one can forget that terrible time."

He continued, "I very much would like to hear your story sometime when you are up to it." and added, "I had to do some research for a school paper and I read that the Nazi German troops invaded Greece during the Second World War."

She nodded her head and said, "Yes, I was three years old when they came. I was too young to understand but I felt my world changing around me."

By that time his sister, 28-year-old Elie, short for Electra, had joined them together with their two younger cousins, Georgie, 18 and Madi, 15. They all enthusiastically entered the conversation asking their Grandmother questions, urging her to tell them her story.

The ever spirited and eager Madi leaned close to her grandmother touching her cheek with her fingers affectionately and said:

"How about writing your story, Grandma? This way all of us could read it," and turning to the others said, "Isn't that a neat idea?

We could print it and each one of us can have a copy. I think it's a great idea."

Her grandchildren's voices stayed with her for the rest of the evening.

Preparing for bed, Madi's last words echoed in her ears; "Why don't you write your story Grandma?" "What a silly idea," she whispered to herself. "How can I write a story like this after so long at my age. I have probably forgotten most of it."

She laid down on the soft bed next to Anthony who was snugly settled on his side of the bed. "Good night honey and Happy Birthday again," he said and puckered up for a kiss." "Have a good and restful night."

She plumped up her pillows behind her back and reached for her reading glasses. She had a great historical fiction novel to read.
She could not concentrate though. She read the words but they had no meaning. She closed her book, turned off the light and shut her eyes determined to fall asleep. She needed her rest.

But her mind was not at peace. In the dark, she kept going back to the recesses of her brain where her past dwelled. Images of the little girl she used to be emerged.

Her parents, their cozy home, her family. Then pictures of the war appeared, the bombs, the sirens, the terror. She saw high green mountains and the familiar warm feeling resurfaced remembering her beloved village Rovoliari.

It was hopeless. She was too keyed up to sleep.
She tossed the bedcovers aside and got out of bed.
Anthony did not stir, "Good, he won't even notice I
am gone"; she chuckled silently. She put her
slippers on, grabbed her cane and shuffled
out of the bedroom shutting the door softly.

She turned on all the lights in the living room and
walked towards her small desk by the window
across the room. She sat down and turned on her
laptop. The brightly lit screen blinded her and she
closed her eyes for a minute.
"Dear God," she prayed, "What am I doing in the
middle of the night? Have I lost my mind?"
She touched the keys with her arthritic fingers
and a strange feeling, a surge of energy came
through her fragile body.
She straightened up her shoulders and began to
write.

Magda Demou-Gryparis

The Story

It was the ominous year of 1941 in Greece. The year of defeat, desperation, starvation and death. The first year of the Nazi German occupation when Greece, after bravely defending its borders against the attack of the Italian army on the Albanian border, finally bowed under the ruthless and mighty German army.

I was just three years old then. For many children, the first years of their lives are happy and carefree in the safety of their home and family, but not for us Greek children living on the onset of a war.

My memories of the earliest years of my life are of the explosions at the nearby German army factory, as bombs were dropped nightly by Allied airplanes.
We would wake up in the middle of the night to the ear-piercing sirens, jump out of our warm beds, grab blankets and warm clothes and rush out the door.

We would crawl along the wall of the house then across to the opening of the shelter and run down the steep dirt steps as fast as we could.

When my father realized that the Nazi German occupation of Greece was imminent, he started digging a bomb shelter in our yard which was not in the back of the property but actually in the front, adjacent to the fence along the side of the street. He dug deep into the earth.

There were many, almost vertical steps that took one down to a small and narrow walkway. On both sides of this passage, on the earthen walls, he had hollowed out four small and cramped recesses which we used for beds whenever we needed to find cover.

He had also dug out another nook at the far end of the shelter for our storage of heavy blankets, extra warm clothes, water, food, candles anything that we might need in case we had to spend long hours underground.

It was damp and very cold in there especially during nighttime when the Allied airplanes always chose to strike. We spent the long hours freezing, praying and waiting for the bombing to end.

It was such a relief to hear the sirens again, letting us know that the air raid was over and we could come out of that cave and return to our beds.

I can still hear the loud, wailing sound of the sirens.

Normally children at that tender age don't have very clear memories of what happens around them, but these were not normal times. These events were deeply imprinted in the children's minds even more than the adults'.

I can still remember details that even my parents could not recall later.
The anxiety we saw on our parents' faces became fear in our hearts. The despair of the adult was transformed into terror in the mind of the child.

Anxiety and terror were impressed upon us so early in our lives that we still feel it and cannot forget. These feelings have shaped our lives forever.

My family lived in Athens, the capital city of Greece. My parents Vasilis and Ekaterini, (Katina, for short) my brother Thanasis, who was seven years old and myself, just three years old.

My father had a good and profitable profession. He and his partner had their own business laying mosaic floors and they provided well for their families. We had everything we needed and we were a happy, loving family.

When the war broke and the German army occupied our country, our world- as everybody else's world around us- was turned upside down. Suddenly my father was out of work. All businesses and schools shut down. When the little savings we had was spent, there was nothing left but four hungry mouths.

As soon as the triumphant enemy troops entered the city of Athens, they seized all food distribution centers and blockaded all roads leading to the city, thus cutting off all food supplies. They took all crops from the farmers for their own use. They looted the stores and warehouses and left the people of Athens trapped in the city to starve.

My father desperately looked everywhere for work, for food, for help.
Everyone we knew was in the same situation. Everyone around us was looking for the same, work, food and help. But there was nothing.

Life in the city was terribly dangerous during that bleak time.

Our lives were in danger day and night, from the
Germans around us, from the Allied bombs being
dropped nightly, and worst of all from the famine
which killed thousands of Athenians that terrible
first year of the occupation. Many food stores shut
their doors and kept their supplies for their own
use. Others were selling their stock on the black
market. Those were the profiteers who came out
rich after the war.

People were trading their belongings, jewelry,
clothes, even their houses. You could trade your
gold ring for a bag of corn meal. There was no
flour to make bread, no oil and no fuel to cook
with. Everyone went up to the surrounding
countryside to pick wood to use for cooking.

My mother once managed to find a handful of
chicken feed, mixed it with water, baked it over a
wood fire and made a thin slab of make believe
bread for us. We pretended it was bread and ate
it.
There were long lines of haggard, hungry people
waiting for hours hoping to get some food,
anything, for their table.
Children, especially boys would wait patiently
outside the hotels where the German officers
stayed and ate, to scrounge any scraps of food
that the hotel employees dumped in the trash
cans outside.

Potato peels were the favorite and the lucky boy would run home proud to be the provider of his family's meal. His mother would boil the potato peels in plenty of water and make a very watery soup with a potato flavor.

I remember well the times the four of us walked along the railway tracks near our neighborhood to find some coal dropped from the trains. We would use it for heating during the winter. We had to be there on time, just as the train was passing to make sure we would find coal before anyone else.
It was a familiar sight seeing people bent over the tracks carrying a bucket looking for coal.

There was a story that my mother used to say of me that happened at a time during the worst periods for our family, when some days we did not have anything to eat.
I begged her to give me two olives to eat for dinner. She asked why and I answered, "Olives are salty, mama, they will make me thirsty; then I will drink lots of water to fill me up and not hear my stomach growling during the night."

For all these reasons, my father had to do something to save his family from certain death. He decided to take us away from the city to Rovoliari, his birthplace, a small village in the central part of Greece. He was 42 years old then.

My father was born in Rovoliari in 1901. He was the oldest male child, so traditionally he was destined to take care of his family. He also had to support his siblings and provide for his sister's dowry and marriage.

When he was nine years old his parents sent him away to find work and send money back home. He joined a group of other people from the village who were going to Constantinople, today's Istanbul, Turkey, to seek work. Greece at that time was too poor to provide jobs for its people and Constantinople was the land of opportunity.

He walked out of his village carrying his good shoes over one shoulder and a bundle of warm bread, cheese and freshly baked squash pita over the other. The burden of the nine-year-old boy's responsibilities weighed heavily on his thin shoulders.

He found work in a grocery store owned by a fellow Greek and he slept in the storage room in the back of the store on empty potato sacks.

He lived and worked there for six years. At fifteen he was tall for his age, strong and healthy.

At that time, the Turkish military was recruiting young men and especially Greek young men into their army. One day while my Dad was out delivering supplies, Turkish soldiers strode into the store and asked for him. His boss told them that he was out delivering supplies. They said they would be back for him.

When my Dad returned to the store his boss told him to leave and find a place to hide. He grabbed his few belongings and started running.

He ran all the way to the harbor where he jumped into a Greek fishing boat. He hid in there until it sailed for the Greek mainland.

When he reached Greece, his first stop was his beloved village. My grandmother Eugenia told us this story, of how my father arrived in Rovoliari, that evening. He knocked on the door of his family's humble home. His mother opened the door, stared at him, but she could not place him so she said, "Who are you, stranger?" His sister who came up behind her mother said, "Mana, don't you know who he is? He is your son Vasilis."

He had left when he was nine and now he returned as a young man of 15. He had grown and changed so much that his own mother did not recognize him.

He stayed with his family for a few months enjoying their comforting love and care that he had missed all those years in a foreign country away from them. He knew, though, that he had to leave again to go out in the world, find work and continue providing for his family.
He went to Athens and through the help of a fellow villager found temporary work.

In 1920, the Greco-Turkish war started. My father, 19 years old then, was drafted and sent to the front to Turkey. Almost two years later after the Greek army was defeated by Kemal Ataturk's fierce soldiers, my father returned to his homeland for good this time.

He served in the police force for a few years and then he was hired by a distant relative from his village, a contractor of mosaic floors who later made him his partner. Through the years my father often visited his village and after he met my mother and they married, he took her to Rovoliari to meet his family and all the loving and generous people of the village.

In my mother's words, " When we reached the top of the hill across from the village I stood speechless. Its beauty enthralled me and right then and there I fell in love with Rovoliari."

This love for "her village" as she called it, continued until the end of her life at the age of 93. So now, in the fall of 1941, my father was going back home to find shelter among the familiar and beloved mountains, his family and all his friends and relatives - the humble people who knew how to give support and love to one of their own.

He knew that Rovoliari being so remote in the midst of high, wooded mountains where its people lived isolated and almost cut off from the rest of the country would be the only solution to our needs. The Germans would not bother with such an insignificant, inaccessible, little village and the Allies, therefore, had no reason to drop their bombs.

We had many relatives there, people who would welcome us and help us. There was also the family land, small fields which belonged to the family and where my parents could farm and grow food.

My mother welcomed his decision to leave but she feared for our home and its contents. An empty house, in a city in the middle of a famine, would definitely be a target for every hungry man to break in and steal anything that could be traded for food.

On the other hand, she knew that if we stayed, she herself would be forced to sell our valuables to provide our family with some sustenance.
I never knew what precious belongings my parents had to part with to fund this move for train tickets, hire mules for transportation and food. I can very well guess that one of them was my father's wedding band because I don't remember seeing it on his finger ever again.

My mother was fortunate to have saved hers because of a kind- hearted doctor in Athens later when I became ill. His name was Dr. John Melas and when my mother offered him her wedding ring for payment, he refused to take it saying that he became a doctor to help people.

We prepared our house for a long absence. We put locks on every closet, drawer and trunk, and taped all the window panes and mirrors with heavy adhesive tape to protect them from breaking during the air raids. After the war was over, those tapes could not be removed and they stayed on for years to remind us of that dismal time. Eventually we had to replace all the window glass and mirrors.

After obtaining a traveling permit we began our preparation for our long journey.

We packed all our valuables, blankets and plenty of warm clothes for the heavy winter months ahead of us among the mighty mountains of Fthiotitha.

We said goodbye to relatives, friends and neighbors and boarded the northbound train.

I do not remember that train trip well, but the story was repeated over and over through the years by my parents. I only remember the people, so many people. The train was so crowded that we were packed one on top of the other.

We traveled for most of the day. The train was very slow.

It stopped at every large or small station and every German checkpoint. It was overflowing with people. Some were moving to safer places, others were moving closer to families and a great number of soldiers were going home. In the middle of all that throng, a small family of four full of hope sought to find a safe hideaway to wait out the war.

Our destination was the small town of Lianokladi, where we got off.

We hired mules to take us to St. George, a large village where my father's uncles and cousins were expecting us. They welcomed us with great joy.

I vaguely remember a cozy room lit by a huge fireplace where we all sat getting warm and enjoying the company.

Our cousins were anxious to hear about the war situation, how things were in the city and how the Germans treated our people. They were appalled at what was happening in Athens and the terrifying and brutal punishments the conquerors were inflicting upon its citizens.
After much talking we all went to sleep by the fireplace covered by warm blankets that smelled of fresh cedar.

Early the next morning after a breakfast of sweet, warm milk, bread and goat cheese we headed for the mountains.
My father had changed plans and decided that instead of going straight to Rovoliari we should visit his mother first, my grandmother Eugenia, who lived in Pitsota a small mountain village three hour away from St. George, climbing over the mountain trails.

My grandfather had passed away two years before and soon after, the family home in Rovoliari was burned down. My grandmother was left homeless so she had to go back to her birth village to live with her sister, Kostando.

It was early October and cold. Winter comes early at that high altitude.

My grandmother was happy to see us and both sisters welcomed us into the warm house, prepared a simple but hearty meal for us and gave us a warm bed to sleep in.

My grandmother, a rough, mountain woman in her seventies had had a hard life. She had worked in the family land all her life, since she was a young girl. She had lost two children, lost her husband and her home in Rovoliari. Her three surviving children all lived in Athens and she was hoping that someday she would move there and live with them.

I have very few memories of my grandmother during that time we spent in Pitsota but one memory will stay with me forever.

I remember going with her to gather walnuts from the huge walnut trees surrounding the village.

She would take long sticks and shake the heavy branches loaded with the rich, delicious nuts and I would run around on my tiny, skinny legs gathering them in my skirt screaming with delight. It was so exciting for me to be in such a place for the first time, with a grandmother so unique and fascinating.

She was a strong and agile woman. She could still do chores that she used to do when she was young. She could also be a cranky, moody, and sharp-tongued woman.

I so vividly remember one morning when she took me with her to pick walnuts from one special tree--she said--that had the largest walnuts. She carried two bags, one to hold her own walnuts and the other one for the rest of us. After picking the walnuts, on the way back home she met a neighbor and stopped to talk to him. For a while I tried to listen to their conversation but I could not understand their mountain dialect and started looking around to find something to occupy myself with. I spotted the two bags of walnuts my grandmother had dropped on the ground. Without realizing I took her bag. I picked up a rock and started cracking the walnuts and eating them. It seems they were talking for a long time because, by the time they finished I had eaten almost half the bag. When grandma Eugenia saw what I had done she turned red from anger and began scolding me. I, frightened and in tears, ran home to my mother.

There was a big argument. Grandma accusing me of eating her walnuts, my mother offering her ours to replace the ones I ate, and grandma refusing to take them, insisting that she wanted hers.
She demanded that I should be punished.

Soon after, we prepared to leave Pitsota for our final destination, Rovoliari.

Winter was upon us and the mountain paths would be treacherous.
We were faced with a slow and hazardous journey of many hours in the forest. My mother had developed an eye infection which was going to make our travel even more difficult and slow.

Once more, we took the trail up and through the high, wooded mountains. The peaks and the slopes were covered with a thick, white carpet of snow.
I was riding a mule most of the time but I remember the experience of walking in the cold snow for the first time in my young life.
There is a picture in my mind of my mother holding on to my father's hand who was guiding her because she could not see through all this whiteness around her. She was wearing a light color coat, almost white, and she seemed like a figure out of a fairy tale book.

My brother was holding on to the mule's tail tightly so he would not stray off the path.
For us children, it was a new experience to climb up and down the mountain slopes. Sometimes we competed with each other, who would leave the deepest footprints in the snow. Many times my father came to my rescue, pulling me out of the holes my little feet made in the deep snow.

It took us almost a full day to reach our destination, Rovoliari. It was a miracle that we were not attacked by wolves. These mountains teemed with wild animals which sometimes raided the villages looking for food.

It was dusk when we reached the last turn of the path on top of the village which we could not see because of the thick layer of fog and snow covering the lower part of the mountain slopes and the rooftops of the houses.

My father said that he knew we had arrived from the barking of the village dogs. Though we were tired and weary we sped down the path as fast as we could to reach the houses and find a shelter. We were so relieved and so hopeful to have finally reached our haven.

Aunt Evthoxia, my father's cousin, her husband and her two young boys, Ilias and Thanasis, welcomed us with open arms. They were expecting us for weeks. They were afraid that we might have gotten lost or maybe had been killed by wolves.

That small house seemed like heaven, after our long and exhausting journey. Aunt Evthoxia served us trahana, a delicious hot homemade soup, with thick-crusted slices of home baked bread and fresh goat's cheese.

It was the most delicious and hearty dinner I had ever tasted.

She gave us their best room, the one saved for guests. Soon, the fragrant wood was burning in the fireplace and was heating up the room. For the first time after so long I saw my father's worried eyes soften and relax. His family was safe and he could hope again.

The large bed welcomed us and we fell asleep under the warm, heavy, wool blankets.

It was a happy awakening the next morning by the loud crowing of the early roosters one after the other all over the village. It sounded to me as if they were competing with each other, wishing us a good morning and telling us "Wake up, a new day is starting".

On that first day in Rovoliari, a new world opened before my eyes. The high mountains surrounded the small village on every side. The stone houses were nestled among ancient tall trees. There was smoke coming out of every chimney and the narrow paths between the houses covered with snow and ice. People were rushing up and down the steep paths, bundled up in their heavy winter coats covering their faces against the freezing wind.

All these new experiences, the new smells, the new noises, the bells from the sheep, the barking of the dogs and the villagers' voices coming from the neighboring houses, fascinated me. I think that was the moment that Rovoliari stole my heart.

It was winter and there were not many things my brother and I could do but I still remember the cold and the whiteness of the snow everywhere. Most of the time I was busy playing with my cousins or following my aunt around the house and down the cellar when she went to feed the animals. My favorite pastime was to watch her knead the bread with her strong rough hands, and then fetch wood to light the fire in the fireplace to bake it. The delicious aroma of the baking bread filled the house. There is nothing like a slice of hot freshly baked bread.

We did not stay long with our cousins. We moved to a house we had rented from a relative, a short distance from my aunt's house.

I remember a large room with a large fireplace taking up one wall. My mother always kept the fire on to heat up the room and to cook our meals. My parents chose this room for all of us to sleep in because it was the warmest room of the house. My bed was between the fireplace and the door and I still remember how snug I was, being so near the fire.

My parents were busy storing the crops which our relatives, who were taking care of our small plots of land, had harvested the previous summer and fall.

That year had not been a good one though. There had not been enough rain the previous spring and the harvest was poor. The wheat, corn and beans would not last us through the winter. My father said that it looked like God had abandoned Greece that year, first with the German troops occupying our country and second with the poor harvest.

Still, he believed he made the right decision to leave the dangerous life of the city.

I, being so young and carefree, was enjoying myself. My favorite playtime was to slide on the snow from the back of the house down to the thick wall of blackberry bushes near the edge of the yard. If there were no bushes I could have found myself falling down the steep drop to the river below.

My carefree days did not last long. As my mother often repeated to me, "On the 26th of October, on St. Demetrios' Day, you fell ill".

Saints' name days are very important and are celebrated throughout Greece, more so in villages where people are deeply devout. These days are holidays for everyone. There is no work and no school.

The people start that big day by putting on their good Sunday clothes and go to church at the first pealing of the church bell.

After the service, they gather in the church yard greeting each other, the men drinking coffee or the local drink, tsipouro. The women and children prefer a sweet loukoumi.

The custom was that everyone was invited to visit the houses of each celebrant to wish them a Happy Name Day. The lady of the house served their home-made pastries or sweet preserves.

Quite often, the guests were invited to stay for lunch, a big feast which lasted for hours. After eating tons of food, drinking lots of glasses of homemade wine, the singing and dancing would start and last long into the night.

Everyone was in high spirits on their way home. It was such a happy holiday, on that particular St. Demetrios' day, that my family joined the rest of the villagers to the church service followed by the feast celebration at a relative's house. By nightfall, my father who was carrying me in his arms on the way home noticed that I was very warm.
Indeed, that day I became very ill with very high fever.

My mother always said that God protected me because a distant relative who was a doctor had just arrived at the village with his family to wait out the war like us. He quickly examined me and announced that I had typhoid fever. He said it was serious and that I had to have injections.

Typhoid is a deadly disease and even deadlier when you are in a remote mountainous village in the middle of a war.

Uncle John, another cousin of my father's, who had served as a medic during the last war, offered to give me the injections. But I needed medicine and the nearest pharmacy was in Makrakomi, a town many hours of walking away, over the mountains.

My brave and devoted father, spent most of the winter months trudging up and down the mountains in the deep snow and freezing temperatures in that high altitude to get my medicine, each time carrying a load of some kind of food to trade for the medicine. Sometimes it was eggs, other times a chicken, freshly made goat cheese or walnuts and chestnuts which were plentiful in our village.

My parents said later that any provisions and food we had stored in the fall was depleted during my illness. My pious mother said that we were in God's hands, He would provide for us and He did. Our relatives and fellow villagers did not let us starve during that time. A cousin baked our bread, a dear old aunt would bring us fresh eggs, a neighbor brought fresh milk and cheese and other food stuff.

I still remember the thick slice of sugared bread that the doctor's wife sent every day for me to have some nourishment.

That's how my father spent that winter walking to Makrakomi and back. His only companion was a mule borrowed from a kind relative.

He made the same trip several times, each time bringing the medicine for the injections my uncle John was giving me. My parents said that if it were not for dear uncle John I would not have survived.

In later years, when I took the same route by bus, I always wondered how my father managed that trip under those difficult conditions.

For months, I was fighting for my life, in high fever, delirious, raving. I had nightmares, one in particular I had over and over. I saw rats crawling all over my bed and my body, biting me, and I would wake up screaming and tearing at my nightshirt. My poor mother would come to my bed to soothe me, assuring me that there were no rats eating me.

She kept mending that nightshirt until I could not wear it anymore.

It was a miracle that I was able to survive such a serious disease under the primitive conditions we lived in then, but slowly I started to improve.

My illness lasted five months. It was spring when I began to feel better and stronger. The first time I tried to get out of bed and stand up, I fell onto the floor.

My little, skinny legs were so weak that they could not support me.
It was on the twenty fifth of March that I was well enough to leave the house. It was another religious holiday and all four of us went to church that morning. My parents lit a candle and offered their tears and thanks to God for my recovery.

Spring in those mountains is glorious, awesome. The haze covering the mountain tops surrounding the village is lifted and the trees start to show their green colors. The first color you see around the village and on the slopes, is the splendid koutsoupia, a flowery tree of gorgeous lavender blossoms.

The blue sky and the bright sun warm the people's hearts after the long winter months. It fills them with hope, joy and energy. The people are ready to start another round of communication with the earth.

They get busy bringing out their plows, hoes and spades to start the new year's cultivation. They till and dig and prepare the soil for the wheat, corn, beans and other crops necessary for their family's yearly food supply.

It is hard work because Rovoliari is built on the sloping sides of the mountain densely covered with a canopy of trees of every kind. Every clearing open to the sky is used for farming, but still it is steep and must be dug by hand. For that reason, the families owned plots of land away from the village in flat areas, sometimes on the top of other mountains miles away.

My father's family owned a small field on a hill across from our house and at dawn each morning my mother and father walked through the winding path, across the stream that split the village in half, then climbed up the steep trail carrying their hoes and picks on their shoulders.

They used them to break the hard soil and get it ready for sowing. After it was planted, they waited and prayed for the spring rains to come.

My brother Thanasis, and I would join them to have lunch when they had a break in the middle of the day. That steep, winding path to the field was frightening to me. It was narrow, thick with trees and bushes on both sides and I always kept close to my brother as we walked.

But my playful brother liked to tease me and scare me. He let me walk on ahead of him, then hid behind some tall ferns and when I could not hear his footsteps or see him when I turned around, I would start crying calling his name. Other times he would throw rocks all around me to scare me even more.

Then, he would creep up on me roaring like a lion.

One day when he played that trick again I decided to be brave and continued walking. He did not like that so he started throwing rocks at me. One of them, a big size stone hit me on the back of my head.

I howled from pain, blood was running down my neck and I was crying and calling my mother. My parents heard my loud screams and came running down the path. It was my brother's turn now to be scared; he got the spanking he deserved.

My father stopped the bleeding by applying scrapings from his leather belt and tied his white shirt around my head. I looked like a wounded soldier coming back from the war.

From that day, every time we scrambled up the hill to meet our parents my brother would walk next to me holding my hand. He did not try to scare me again.

I still have the scar on the back of my head to remind me of those long ago unforgettable days.

As spring was turning into summer my parents were pleased to see their work and their hopes becoming real.

The wheat field turned green as the tiny blades started to grow. The corn and the vegetables also flourished. We were going to have a good harvest that year.

Mother and father continued to walk up the hill at dawn tending the field, hoeing and weeding, while my brother and I were discovering new adventures.

My brother liked to climb trees and many of these were fruit trees, which by that time were full of spring blossoms. I tried to imitate him but I stayed away from the cherry trees. My mother said that cherries were her favorite fruit and told us not to climb the cherry trees so we would not break the fragile pink blossoms and since mother liked cherries, I was sure I would love them also.

In late May and early June, the cherries were starting to ripen and ready to be picked. The villagers helped each other harvesting the delicious fruit. Some would climb up the trees having baskets tied around their waists with ropes and when the baskets were full of the red juicy fruit they lowered them to the ground where others loaded them on donkeys.

The women were particularly happy because they made their delicious cherry preserves, sweets and refreshing drinks.

As the days grew warm, we children were always scampering around the village, climbing a hill, dropping by the house of a welcoming relative, looking for a treat of walnuts or chestnuts, picking fruit from a wide variety of trees, or visiting the various little churches that were scattered all over the village.

Other times, we would climb steep paths to reach various natural springs, to drink their refreshing icy cold water. There were many such natural springs in and around the village and each one of them had names: Dibla, Megali, Solina.

Very often we would bring along some snack to eat sitting next to the trickling water. Food tasted better there. Afterwards we would fill the large flask my brother carried with him and take it home.

My grandmother Eugenia who had joined us in Rovoliari by then, liked to take my brother Thanasi on little excursions to various places around the village, especially when the fruit were ripe for picking. She showed us where the sweetest plums were, the most fragrant pears and especially the mulberries.

One Sunday afternoon, after church, she asked us to go with her to a mulberry tree that had the largest and sweetest fruit.
That huge mulberry tree belonged to the family and it was next to the empty lot where the family home used to be before it was burned down.
My mother let us go after we promised that we would be careful not to stain my pretty, bright, yellow dress she had made for me.
Grandma was hitting the branches with her walking stick to shake the fruit down while my brother and I were picking them and eating them as they were dropped on the ground. They were big, magenta red, sweet and sour, delicious mulberries.

My brother was not satisfied with the few we were able to pick so he climbed up the tree and started picking and eating. I, from below, was yelling for him to drop some for me and he answered, "hold up your skirt to keep them from falling on the ground," and I did. I had my fill of the juiciest mulberries I ever had in my life but my beautiful new dress was ruined.
Mother had a fit when we got home.

Sometimes in the warm afternoons, we would spread a blanket under the cool shade of a tree by the stream, listening to the song of the cicadas, pretending to rest.

I loved everything in the village but most of all I liked the mornings we spent by the cool river on washing days.
We would take the narrow path among the brambles and blackberry bushes leading down to the river.

We helped our mother by bringing dry twigs and wood from the steep and rocky banks of the stream for kindling to start the fire at the edge of the water. She filled a large kettle with water from the river and let it get very hot. Then she scooped in ashes from the fire to make the water soft and whiten the clothes.

She dipped the laundry in, left them in for a few minutes. She then took them out and using a homemade bar of soap, lathered them and beat them against the flat rocks.

Afterwards she rinsed them well in the clear cold mountain water and spread them on the nearby bushes and hedges to dry.

While waiting for the clothes to dry my brother and I would take off our shoes and step into the freezing stream looking for crabs. I just followed him and every time I saw him with a crab in his hand, I would screech with excitement.

My brother was clever at finding them under the rocks; he was never afraid of picking them up. Later, we helped our mother pick up the dry clothes and headed back home, with my brother carrying a bag with his live trophies.
Our grandmother showed us how to roast the crabs.
She would take the hard-homemade bread, remove the crust, sprinkle it with olive oil, salt, pepper and plenty of aromatic oregano picked from the same mountain where the river was running through.
Then she cut the crabs open and filled them with the bread stuffing and roasted them under the hot coals in the kitchen fireplace.

It was a happy and carefree time for me, because I was in a beautiful world, a world I had not seen before. I did not have any toys, for me the whole world was my toy. The mountains around me, the old stone houses nestled among the ancient trees, all this green magic that surrounded me.
Everyday there were new things to discover, new things to play with.

When evening came, complete darkness covered the small village.
This darkness was absolute, solid. No light was escaping from the houses. During those times, the people used oil lamps and carried them from room to room.

The only light came from the starry sky on clear nights.
When there was a moon, we could see it only for a short time when it reached the sky between the two mountains that enclosed the village.
This darkness scared me.
On the warm summer nights, we would move our bedding outdoors to the balcony which was small but just big enough for the four of us. I always slept close to my father for protection.
It was beautiful but frightening at the same time.
All night, you could hear strange noises from the night creatures who came out after dark.

We could hear the howling of the wolves coming from high up the mountain slopes, heard the more daring hungry jackals who came closer to the village and the owl that seemed to be right there on the roof of the house. Sometimes we could hear the panicky cackling of the chicken from a nearby coup when a cunning fox would try to get them.

But Gioni was the most frightening of all for me! Gioni is a night bird and the people gave it that name because of the sound it makes. It sounds like a cry.
This story has come down through the ages, a lore that people repeated over and over.

It is said that there was a man looking for his younger brother named Yianni who had been lost in the woods up high up in the mountains.
The older brother blamed himself for his brother's disappearance and he was searching for days and nights but could not find him. So, after many days of looking for him he prayed to God and begged Him to turn him into a bird so he could fly over the trees and the mountain peaks to find his brother. God pitied him and made him a bird. Ever since, he comes out at night, flies over the forest calling his brother. Gion, Gion.

It is an eerie, haunting sound that makes your skin crawl and for a little girl hearing this in the night surrounded by this blackness, was terrifying. Every time I heard it, I would cover my head with the blanket and reach for my Daddy's comforting arms.

As summer was getting warmer, it was time for the wheat harvest. We would all wake up at dawn and after a quick breakfast of bread and milk, we would take the winding path uphill to the wheat field. My parents would start the back-breaking work of reaping the golden tall stalks using long sharp sickles, cutting with one hand while holding the dry wheat stalks with the other.

My brother was put to work too, by gathering the reaped stalks, putting them together in bundles and leaving them on the ground for my parents to bind later.
I wanted to join them but I was too little for this kind of work. My mother showed me how to pick the leftover stalks and put them on top of the bundles. I was struggling behind them, panting and sweating, never being able to catch up with them. Soon I would get tired and look for the shade of a tree to rest.

We spent a few days on the wheat field.

When all the wheat was harvested and bundled up, it was left on the field to dry in the hot sun. Later, it was loaded up on donkeys and carried to the aloni, the threshing floor. This was a round dirt area on a small flat hill, near the village, laid with tiles or packed hard with animal dung and smoothed over so that the surface was level and shiny and left to dry. It was well kept and maintained by the villagers.

There was a tall wooden pole embedded in the middle. The dry bundles of wheat were spread on this surface around the pole.
Then, a couple of mules or bulls were tied on the pole by a long rope. The animals were forced to walk around the pole first one direction and then the other. This way, while they walked, they crushed the dry wheat with their hoofs.

My father was put to the task of walking behind a mule urging it to walk around the pole.
After many hours of treading on the dry grain under the hot sun my father was happy to join us under the cool shade of a nearby tree and lunch on hard bread, cheese and olives, the soul food of the Greek peasant and drink the crispy, cool spring water of the village. At the end of the day we were so exhausted, we could hardly walk back to the house across the hill.

After the tedious work of threshing was done everybody would take long, handmade, wooden forks and start tossing the crushed stalks up in the air for the grain to separate from the stalks and drop on the ground. It had to be a breezy day to do that. Afterwards, the stalks were removed and the grain was swept with brooms and put into burlap bags. The wheat was ready to be loaded on the donkeys and taken to the mill to be ground into flour.

When the hardest of the summer work was over, my parents were relieved and happy. Their hard work had paid off and they were hoping the flour would last us for many months.
Still, there was more work to be done.

The summer months in the village were the most productive and hardworking months of the whole year.
The villagers labored from dawn to dusk. It was harder for the women because their work would continue till the late hours of the night.
All the houses were empty during the day, except for the old who were not strong enough for field work. The chickens could be heard clucking in the yards and the dogs barking and roaming the lanes while guarding the village.

Every family member was out in the fields, watering their gardens, hoeing, picking, gathering, harvesting. When nightfall came, they strode down the hills, the slopes and the paths towards home. You could tell they were coming home by the tinkling of the small bells around their goats' and sheep's necks, because whichever destination they took in the morning, they always took their animals with them to forage in the greenery around.

The women were laden high up on their backs with wood and kindle for the fireplace and some young mothers carried their babies, strapped around their chests. They were always rushing down to light the fires and prepare the evening meal.

The summer months were not just hard work, though. They were months of fun, enjoyment, cheer, getting together, visiting each other and relaxing.

In July, Rovoliari has three celebrations.

The first one is on July 20th, the Prophet Ilias day. The tiny white church of the Prophet Ilias is located on a high mountain peak straight up over the village. It is built on a small plateau in a green valley.

In the spring and summer, this glen is covered with a profusion of wildflowers of all colors. Standing up there, you feel that you are on top of the world.
You look around you and you see near and distant mountain peaks as far as the eye can see; on a clear day you can also make out white villages scattered on far away mountain slopes.

The villagers start up very early in the morning, climbing the steep wooded path with their priest leading the way. Some people guide their donkeys and mules laden with provisions for the feast that will take place after the service.
It's an unforgettable experience to partake in this unique liturgy of St Ilias.

The other two festivities are the St. Paraskevi day on the 26th and the St. Panteleimon day on the 27th. These two days of music and dancing into late hours, which extended to three or four sometimes, were the once a year events that the people waited for throughout the year.
These saints were so important to the villagers, that every household named their son or daughter after their two saints, Paraskevi or Panteli, respectively.
In preparation, houses were aired and cleaned. The women prepared delicious desserts and cooked their best dishes.

Families would reunite with family and friends, open their houses for visiting relatives. Sons and daughters who lived far away would come to see their kinfolk.

People from surrounding villages would walk miles over the mountains to spend a day or two and enjoy this exciting time with other people.

It was also during these festivities that young men and women would meet and fall in love and eventually marry.

That year, we joined in the celebrations. We went to the church services in the morning and afterwards we enjoyed the festivities held in the church yard. The food was plentiful. Whole lambs sprinkled with aromatic herbs on spits, were roasted over the hot coals in pits.

Savory pites and appetizing dishes made by the village women lay on tables and everyone was drinking the strong wine and the sweet smelling tsipouro.

The local musicians with their clarinet, fiddle and laouto, played and sang the popular folk music of the people of the land, all through the days and nights. The mountains surrounding the village were reverberating with the sound of their revelry.

The villagers enjoyed such occasions as the Saint's days and they loved to hike many miles to other distant villages to join in their own celebrations. It was during the summer months that the residents of the various villages and towns would visit each other, communicate and exchange news.

In late summer, the delicious grapes ripened, ready to be picked. Each family made their own home-made wine, stored it in wooden barrels and kept it in their cool cellars. With the leftover grape skins and clippings, they made a local aromatic and strong drink called tsipouro, similar to moonshine.

It was my grandmother's favorite. During cold winter nights, she heated it up over the fire, added a little sugar and sipped it slowly.
It was her medicine for a cold or aching bone, she used to say. She called it ponchi. There were times when while heating it, it caught on fire, that's how strong it was.

When the corn was ready to be harvested, the whole village got into an energetic fervor. Corn was the second most important food after the wheat for their survival.
A good harvest of corn meant a year of plenty for the families. It meant corn breads, pitas, sweet pastries and food for their animals all year.

This time, the villagers would help each other with the picking and bringing the corn to their individual houses.

They dumped the ripe corn on their balcony floor or on the dirt floor of their yard and left it to dry to be husked.

It was so much fun to be part of one of those "husking the corn" evening parties. There was always a bonfire and relatives and neighbors sat around enjoying the fellowship. Delicacies and wine were passed around and everyone joined in, laughing, singing, roasting and eating the sweet grain grown in their own fields, in their own village, in their beloved mountains, by their own strong, callused hands.

Later, the people would have discussions on whose corn husking party was more successful and more fun.

I remember that certain year we joined in aunt Evthoxia's party. The surprise that night, was uncle Demetri's delicious figs from Pipilia an area close to the village where the fruit ripened sooner because of its milder climate.

The sudden bursts of thunder meant fall and the coming of winter. Dark clouds covered the sky over the small village among the wooded slopes.

It was fierce, menacing. The thick layer of fog locally called andara, lifted from the river and the low flat areas, rising high onto the slopes and peaks and heavily covering the trees, the red tiled roofs of the houses, the gardens and the whole village.

Soon, the pouring rain turned the steep dirt paths and trails into small streams running down to the dry river which split the village into two, filling it up and flooding it. The path that connected the two banks of the river in the summer became impassable.

The people of the west bank could not go over to the east bank. Friends and families were cut off from each other for as long as the rain lasted and the water in the river remained high.

Our life in the village was soon to be changed. In the fall of 1942 disturbing news reached our village. Our lives were not going to be peaceful for long. The war was spreading to the countryside all over Greece and it was getting nearer. As the resistance groups were growing and gaining power, they were receding, seeking refuge onto the mountains. The enemy soldiers were following them. We heard reports of fierce battles between the two sides.

Alarming news reached us of whole villages being burned down by the Nazi soldiers, people losing their lives trying to save their animals and their possessions or others fleeing to the higher elevations trying to save themselves and their families.

For my family, the news was a waking up call. My parents realized that we could not stay in the village any longer. We had to leave our safe harbor. We had to return home, back to Athens. Winter was also approaching fast and snow falls heavily upon those mountains. Soon the paths and roads would become inaccessible and blocked. My parents were concerned that if we waited much longer we would not be able to leave the village until next spring. So, they began preparations for our long journey.

Thanks to their hard work the previous spring and summer we had enough provisions to last us for a few months. They hired mules to transport our possessions and food and started the trek down the steep trails.

We made a stop at our cousins' house in the village of St George to say goodbye and headed for Lianokladi to board the train back to Athens.

I remember that train ride. It was crammed with people. Every space was taken. We all had to sit on the floor in the spaces between the seats holding on to each other and our belongings.
The cabin where we were able to find room was full of gypsy families. My mom cautioned us not to sit too close to them because they were known to have lice. It would not be avoided though, as there was no room.

My mother was right. As soon as we arrived home we discovered that we were infested with lice. My mom got to work.
We were stripped off of every stitch of clothing which she dipped into boiling water. But the stubborn lice would not give in, it clung into our hair and none of our mother's ministration would help. She did the only thing left to do. She shaved my and my brother's heads.
There is a picture of me and my brother stiffly looking at the camera in our back yard with shaved heads. It looked normal for my brother but not for me, a girl.
We were relieved to be back home, although my parents discovered that the locks of our closets and drawers were broken and many of my mother's beautiful, handmade and embroidered dowry pieces that she herself had made were gone. Someone had taken them to exchange for food.

The situation in Athens had not changed. The German army was still occupying the city and fear was still rooted in people's hearts. Human life was cheap.

The Nazis were shooting anyone who dared raise their heads to protest or just look at them. The resistance groups were doing a lot of damage to them and the Germans brutally punished the guilty and the innocent alike.

There were rumors that even in our small neighborhood, there was such a resistance group of young men who were meeting in a house just behind ours where they met to listen to the BBC at night and plot their next move against the enemy.

Some people in the neighborhood knew about their secret meetings but kept quiet because spies were everywhere. Everyone was whispering: «Even the walls have ears."

My family was trying to survive in the city. My father tried to find work.

He heard that the nearby army munitions factory, which had been taken over by the German army at the onset of the occupation, needed laborers. He went hoping to be hired. However, my mother was worried and scared knowing that my father would be working so closely with the enemy.

The Germans were known to execute people for no reason at all.

One morning, not long after my father started working at the factory, we heard loud explosions and smoke coming from there.

The residents in our quiet neighborhood, alarmed by the deafening blast, ran outside to investigate. They were looking at each other questioning for news. My mother, my brother and I joined them out in the street.

We all stood there all day, staring anxiously towards the end of our street waiting for father to come home.

Near dusk men started coming up the street but not our Dad. My mother was frantic fearing the worst.

Later that evening we saw him coming. He looked tired, haggard, and could hardly walk.

After he rested and had some nourishment, he was finally able to talk.

He said that after the explosion, the Germans blamed the Greek workers and ordered them into a warehouse and started interrogating them. They were kept in there all day. Some were arrested and the rest were let go. My mother could not stop thanking God for our father's rescue. It was a close call.

Magda Demou-Gryparis

Epilogue

The Nazi German occupation force remained in Greece for almost two more years. By that time, Greece was in ruins. Thousands perished and those remaining were traumatized, exhausted, and hungry, always hungry.
It was a miracle that my family survived these four years of terror and extreme suffering. It was my parents' wise decision to leave the city that saved us.

We never forgot the time we spent in the village. The memory of it always warmed our hearts. We thought of ourselves to be the most fortunate of people to have lived among the purest, most generous and most loving human beings. Truly all these wonderful and kind people saved our lives. My parents never forgot their generosity.

After the war, when most of the villages in the country were destroyed and uninhabited, people started to move to the city as many of our friends and relatives did, to find work.

My parents opened our home and welcomed them. There was always a bed to sleep on and a hot meal for anyone who needed a place to stay. There were times when every room in the house had two or three makeshift beds. Those times I, being the youngest slept on two chairs which my mother made comfortable by spreading thick blankets on the seats.

I never stopped loving the village and its people.

I was thirteen years old when I revisited Rovoliari again and did so every summer after that. As soon as school was out, I would board the train and head for my beloved mountains.
I spent my summers with my aunt Aggelo and my cousins.
Even now, in my old age, after having lived for so many years away from my native country, I still ache for Rovoliari. I still want to see those dear-to- my heart mountains one more time.

In writing these memoirs of the time my family and I spent in Rovoliari, during the war years, I have blended the events of that time, with my later memories and experiences I had every time I visited Rovoliari during the summers I spent there as a teenager.
But that world is gone. It is sad that this thriving, full of life village is no more.

It is still there of course, it is still beautiful and green and mesmerizing, but it is almost empty of its people, of its life. Those proud, hardworking, earth people are missing.
The old people have died, while their children and grandchildren have moved to the cities to make a better living. There are still a few people remaining, those who refuse to move to the cities or those who do not want to abandon the homes of their ancestors.

On important holidays and in the summer, the children and grandchildren return to spend a few cool days in their family homes. Many of those children are maintaining them, making repairs, painting them, and preserving them for the next generations.

Every time I went back, I walked through the overgrown paths and the empty houses, and I could still hear the tinkling of the animal bells, still see the fireside smoke coming out of the chimneys, filling the air with the aroma of the burned cedar, the fresh baked bread, the smell of the animals and the cooking fires, mixed all together, turned all into a unique smell, the smell of unforgettable Rovoliari.

I so much wish I could see my memorable wonderful, spellbinding Rovoliari again but I am no longer able to make this long and difficult journey.

To my Parents

I cannot finish these memoirs without mentioning my beloved parents who were the heroes of this story, during those hard, oppressive and endless war years. By leaving Athens and moving to the village, they knew that their life would become harsher in a primitive mountain community.

They knew they would have to work hard and struggle to survive and to provide the necessities for themselves and their two young children relying on the kindness and generosity of their kin and friends.
It was more difficult for my mother who was not used to that rough lifestyle but proved herself to be a warrior.
She worked relentlessly, tirelessly next to my father, never complaining of the hard labor, and the severe circumstances they lived in.

My mother was born in a village outside Argos, in the Peloponnese peninsula. That village was not as remote and untamed as Rovoliari. From early age, she was exposed to a more refined and worldly lifestyle. She did not toil in the fields.

She loved to read, she did fine and beautiful handiwork. Her embroideries were the finest in her village. She also loved music and she had a beautiful voice.

When she was 15 years old, she was sent to Athens to live as an apprentice in the house of a well-sought-after seamstress in the city, whose clients were part of the high society of Athens.

Because my mother always liked to sing while she was sewing, people started to notice her lovely voice and word spread around.

One day, a tenor from the Opera House heard of a village girl with a magnificent voice and came to the house asking to hear my mother sing. She did without any hesitation or any nervousness.

The musician was impressed and right away sent a letter to my grandfather back in the village, asking his permission to allow his daughter to be trained for the opera.

My grandfather's response was "I sent her to the city to become a seamstress and not a saloon entertainer". Obviously, my grandfather had no idea what an opera house was.

So, my mother had to go back home and stay, hurt and disappointed. I do not believe that she ever forgave her father for stopping her from fulfilling her dream.

Years later, while visiting her older sister in Athens, she met my father and a year later they were married.
She was twenty-nine years old and my father was thirty-two. It was a union blessed by the Gods. Two of the kindest, gentlest, purest in heart people found one another and made each other happy.

My father, being forced to leave his family at a very early age, living a lonely life and my mother, being trapped in her village, while her heart was longing for a better life. They were two lonely human beings waiting for their other half. They, with their two children created a nest of love and devotion to each other.
My brother and I both loved and respected our parents.
I have always been proud of them, for what they were able to achieve in their lives, despite their lack of formal education and their humble beginnings.
They taught us love, respect for each other, honesty, honor, generosity, pride, love for your fellow man and love for learning.

I greatly admired and appreciated my parents for their values and for their gentle and kind hearts.

My Parents

Author's Comments

When I first began to write this story, I felt a strong urge to express my feelings and my love for the village where I spent so many unforgettable summers in my youth. I felt that by writing about those summers, I would relive all those happy experiences.

It was a few years after our small family, my husband, our young son and I left our native country Greece to emigrate to America when I started feeling terribly homesick for my family, my country and all that we had left behind; but the nostalgia for Rovoliari became stronger, even painful.

So, I took pen and paper and started to put down every experience, event and impression I could remember of all the summers I spent in the village as a child and a teenager.

I wrote about its beauty, its wonderful people who welcomed me in their midst and the carefree days I so loved to enjoy under the canopy of its green magnificence.

For a long time, I was satisfied with my writings, but then I realized that they were just memories, sentences with no foundation.

So, I asked myself "How can I use all these feelings and the attraction the village had on me in a story with content, with substance."

Searching through my memory, I went back to the time of the war during the Nazi German occupation when I was very young and the experience and adventure my family lived through when we had to flee Athens and go to Rovoliari to survive. I realized that all these emotions and experiences could be put together and become the basis for a short story or a novella where I could express my feelings and love for the village.

I was worried that I might not be able to recollect details of that war experience being so young then. But as I began writing, I discovered that more and more memories were coming to my mind.

It took me years to write my story and I might not have finished it if it were not for my cousin Ilias Nellas, the editor of Rovoliaritika Nea, urging me to do so. He offered to translate the story into Greek and publish it in the village newspaper.

I am thrilled to have my story published, even in such a small newspaper in Greece.

I feel that I am paying tribute to that small corner of my native country which meant so much to me and my family.

Magda Demou- Gryparis

Magda Demou-Gryparis

About the Author

Magda Demou-Gryparis was born in Athens, Greece during the turbulent years of World War II. She was just three when the Nazi German troops invaded the country. Those four years of aggressive foreign rule had a great impact on her life.

This story is a collection of memories from a year of her young life during the German occupation, during which her family had to escape from the city and find shelter in a mountainous village in Central Greece in order to survive.

In 1967 Magda Demou-Gryparis and her family emigrated to America. Magda is an accomplished artist in oils and watercolors and keeps active by painting and exhibiting her work.

She lives in Madison, Wisconsin with her husband.

Artwork by the Author Magda Demou-Gryparis

"Roumeli Vista" Watercolor on paper.
A scenery from Ftelia, an area near Rovoliari with a spectacular view of the surrounding mountains.

"Rendina Hills" Oil. Spring in the mountains of
Fthiotitha. Spectacular view from
the Monastery of Rendina. The vibrant living
flowers seem to nourish and support the dead
tree on the left.

"Loyal Friend" Oil. A bright sunny day in summer.
A scene of everyday life in the village. The laden
mule carrying supplies to the barn with the
faithful dog at his side.

"Road Home" Watercolor on paper. It's late summer. A woman returning home from the pasture with her goats behind her looking at the spectacular view of the mountain and the village houses spread on the steep slopes.

"Old Misak House" Oil
A traditional old stone village house built by the
villagers themselves using local materials. Some
of them could be 100-200 years old.

Magda Demou-Gryparis

Rovoliari

Magda Demou-Gryparis

Made in the USA
Las Vegas, NV
15 September 2023

77627497R00052